OCT 2 6 2007

The KidHaven Science Library

Predicting Earthquakes

by Peggy J. Parks

KIDHAVEN PRESS
An imprint of Thomson Gale, a part of The Thomson Corporation

THOMSON
™
GALE

Detroit • New York • San Francisco • New Haven, Conn. • Waterville, Maine • London

THOMSON
GALE

Picture Credits:

Cover: Daniel Sambraus/ Photo Researchers Inc.
AP/Wide World Photos, 12, 25, 27, 28, 30
© Bettmann/CORBIS, 5
© Dennis M. Sabangan/epa/CORBIS, 40
© Fabrizio Bensch/Reuters/CORBIS, 36
© Jim Sugar/CORBIS, 19, 38
© Karen Kasmauski/CORBIS, 33
© Lou Dematteis/Reuters/CORBIS, 22
Maury Aaseng, 8
Photos.com, 15
© Reuters/CORBIS, 6
© Roger Ressmeyer/CORBIS, 17, 21
© Tom Bean/CORBIS, 9

© 2007 Thomson Gale, a part of The Thomson Corporation.

Thomson and Star Logo are trademarks and Gale and KidHaven Press are registered trademarks used herein under license.

For more information, contact
KidHaven Press
27500 Drake Rd.
Farmington Hills, MI 48331-3535
Or you can visit our Internet site at http://www.gale.com

LIBRARY OF CONGRESS CATALOGING-IN-PUBLICATION DATA

Parks, Peggy J., 1951–
Predicting earthquakes / by Peggy J. Parks.
    p. cm. -- (Kidhaven science library)
Includes bibliographical references and index.
ISBN 13: 978-0-7377-3602-1 (hardcover : alk. paper)
ISBN 10: 0-7377-3602-X (hardcover : alk. paper)
1. Earthquake prediction—Juvenile literature. I. Title.
QE538.8.P37 2007
551.22--dc22   2006023947

Printed in the United States of America

Contents

Chapter 1

Nature's Violence

During the early-morning hours of May 27, 2006, disaster struck the Indonesian island of Java. Without warning, the ground suddenly began to shake and rumble. The noise was deafening as the heaving earth caused houses, schools, and hotels to crumble. Huge trees snapped as though they were matchsticks, roads buckled, and bridges collapsed into piles of rubble. Then, less than one minute after it began, the rumbling stopped. Java had been struck by an earthquake, one of nature's most violent phenomena.

From Tiny to Massive

Earthquakes like the one in Indonesia always make worldwide news because they are so violent and destructive. But quakes of various strengths occur throughout the world every day. Out of several million earthquakes that occur annually, most are so weak they are not even noticeable. About five hundred thousand are detected each year. Only about a hundred of those are strong enough to cause severe damage.

Scientists rate the severity of earthquakes according to the **Richter scale**. It measures the amount of force behind an earthquake. Small quakes register from 2.0 to 2.9 on the Richter scale. Although they cannot usually be felt, they are detectable by devices known as **seismographs**. Major earthquakes register 7.0 or higher on the Richter scale. These are the powerful quakes that cause the greatest amount of damage.

The most severe earthquake ever recorded registered 9.5 on the Richter scale. It struck the South American country of Chile on May 22, 1960, and killed more than 2,000 people. The quake also triggered an enormous, powerful, fast-moving ocean wave known as a **tsunami**. The tsunami pounded

The Richter scale, used to measure earthquakes, was named for seismologist Charles Richter (pictured).

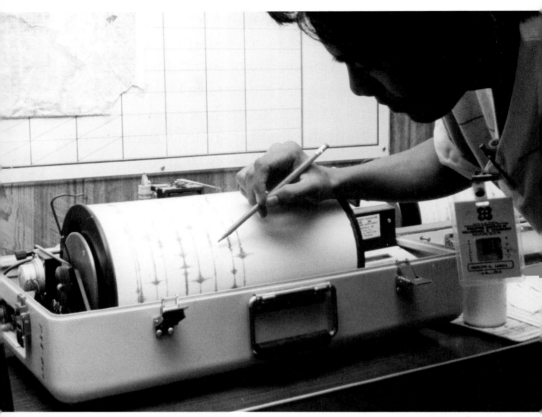

A scientist checks the readings on a seismograph, which detects earthquakes.

coastlines on both sides of the Pacific Ocean with waves up to 50 feet (15m) high—a towering wall of water as high as a five-story building.

An Unsteady Earth

Wherever they occur, all earthquakes are caused by powerful forces deep within the Earth. As rock solid as the planet appears to be, its continents are constantly on the move. This shifting of the continents can be explained by **plate tectonics**.

Plate tectonics is a scientific theory that Earth's **crust** (its rigid top layer) is divided into gigantic slabs of rock known as plates. Much like rafts floating on a lake, the plates float on a churning layer of hot liquid rock known as the mantle. The immense heat deep within the Earth's core provides fuel that keeps the plates constantly adrift. They move very slowly —less than 2.5 inches (6.4cm) per year, which is only about twice as fast as fingernails grow.

Plates can behave in different ways at the boundaries that divide them. Sometimes they move apart, or just slide past each other. They may also head straight toward each other and collide. When there is a collision between two plates, the heavier plate is shoved under the lighter one. This is a process known as subduction.

Faults and Earthquakes

As Earth's plates constantly jostle, grind, and crunch together, they put extreme force on themselves and each other. This can cause huge rocks in the crust to break, creating cracks known as **faults**. As time goes by, the rocks on either side of a fault continue grinding against each other. The pressure from this grinding causes some rocks to be forced upward and others to be forced downward. This motion can drastically change the landscape. The result may be everything from long, curving ridges to towering mountain ranges. South America's majestic Andes Mountains were created by this

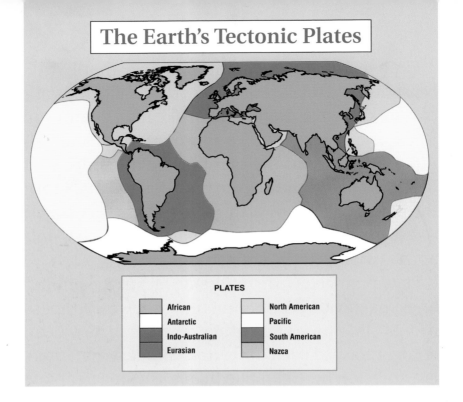

The Earth's Tectonic Plates

PLATES

African
Antarctic
Indo-Australian
Eurasian
North American
Pacific
South American
Nazca

process, as were the European Alps and the Himalayas in Asia.

Faults are not necessarily clean breaks in the crust. A fault may actually be an entire zone hundreds of feet wide. In some areas of the world, there are massive fault zones (also called fault systems). One of the most famous is the San Andreas Fault in California. It stretches for more than 800 miles (1,287km), and in some places it is 10 miles (16km) deep. The San Andreas Fault was created over millions of years as the Pacific Ocean plate and North American plate ground against each other.

Although earthquakes do not always occur in fault zones, they are more common in these places than anywhere else. That is because of the constant

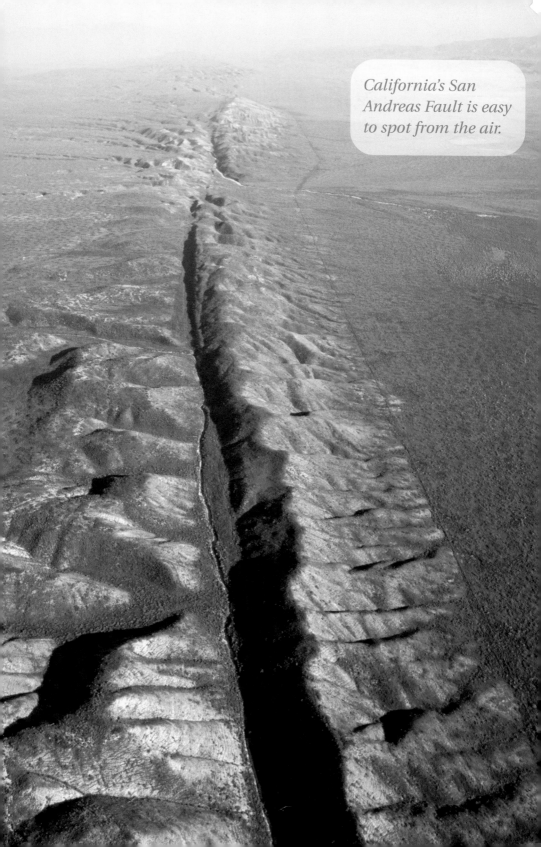

California's San Andreas Fault is easy to spot from the air.

plate movement below the faults. As plates shift, pressure continuously builds up along their boundaries. When the pressure becomes too great, the rocks on either side of the boundaries suddenly shift with great force. Enormous bursts of energy are released and an earthquake is born, as scientist Crystal Wicker explains: "Imagine holding a pencil horizontally. If you were to apply a force to both ends of the pencil by pushing down on them, you would see the pencil bend. After enough force was applied, the pencil would break in the middle, releasing the stress you have put on it. The Earth's crust acts in the same way."[1]

When a sudden break or shift occurs in the crust, **seismic** energy moves outward from the source, known as the **hypocenter**. This energy travels through the Earth in the form of powerful shock waves.

"A Collision Course"

One area that is especially prone to earthquakes is known as the Ring of Fire. Shaped like a giant horseshoe, the Ring of Fire covers thousands of miles. It stretches from the western coast of South America, through the island nations of the South Pacific, and on through Southeast Asia. There are many plate boundaries throughout the area, and it is filled with faults. As a result, as much as 90 percent of the world's earthquakes occur in the Ring of Fire.

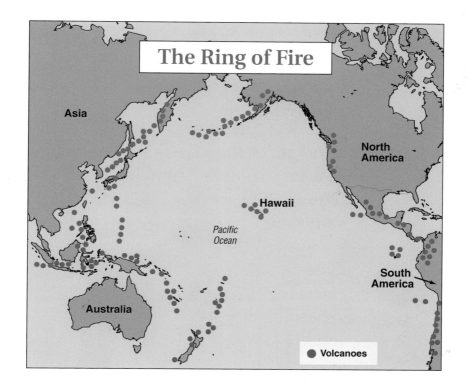

The Ring of Fire

Asia

North America

Hawaii

Pacific Ocean

South America

Australia

● Volcanoes

All the islands that make up Indonesia are located in the Ring of Fire, which is why earthquakes happen so often there. Java's May 2006 quake was caused by the Australian plate pushing under the lighter Sunda plate. Scientists warn that as the two plates continue to grind against each other, more earthquakes will occur. According to the U.S. Geological Survey (USGS), Indonesia is on "a collision course with the northeastward drifting Australian Plate."[2]

Dangerous Wave

A similar plate collision near the Indonesian island of Sumatra caused an earthquake in December

Because of the massive tsunami it triggered, the 2004 Sumatra earthquake was one of the deadliest natural disasters in history.

2004—and it was one of the deadliest natural disasters in history. The widespread destruction was not, however, due to the earthquake itself. It resulted from an enormous tsunami that the quake generated.

The Sumatra earthquake was caused by the collision of the India and Burma plates. These two plates join together about 4 miles (6.4km) beneath the Indian Ocean. They have been bumping into each other for centuries. Finally, the built-up stress and tension became so strong that the lighter Burma plate abruptly snapped upward. The seafloor burst apart, triggering a violent underwater explosion. The seismic energy released in the explosion had the force of several thousand nuclear bombs. All that energy was transferred to the water, causing the deadly tsunami.

A Violent Phenomenon

Earthquakes are some of nature's most violent phenomena. Scientists have learned a great deal about them through the years, but they want to learn much more. If they can better understand the forces behind earthquakes, they will be better equipped to predict where and when quakes are most likely to occur. Science writer Daniel Pendick explains, "As long as earthquakes remain deadly and destructive, we will dream of being able to foresee the next 'big one' coming before it strikes."[3]

Chapter 2

A Challenging Science

Throughout history people have tried to predict earthquakes. They have observed and monitored changes in everything from the atmosphere to groundwater levels. In some countries, people paid close attention to the actions of animals. They were convinced that the creatures could sense tremors in the Earth before humans could. In Japan, for instance, people noticed that catfish became especially active just before an earthquake. They viewed the fish's unusual behavior as a sure sign that a quake was about to strike.

Today most researchers dismiss those beliefs as having no scientific basis. But even scientists have a difficult time predicting earthquakes, and some say it is impossible. Andy Michael, a researcher with the USGS, explains how challenging quake prediction is: "If you know the weather in Kansas today, you can pretty much guess areas a few hundred miles east of Kansas will get that weather tomorrow. . . . Earthquakes happen suddenly; we can't watch the system [develop]."[4] Michael says that one of the biggest problems for scientists is that so much remains unknown. In spite of the knowledge researchers have gained about plate tectonics, the exact processes that control earthquakes are still mysterious.

Ancient Clues

To learn more about those processes, scientists study earthquake activity from the past. This is a branch of science known as **paleoseismology**. It is

People in Japan believe catfish behave strangely right before an earthquake.

valuable because earthquakes often occur in the same place over and over again, as scientist John McCloskey explains: "We have all heard that lightning does not strike twice in the same place—but earthquakes do. . . . Where you have one earthquake you are likely to have others."[5]

Fault Zones

Scientists often focus their studies on Earth's fault zones because that is where earthquakes are most likely to occur. They dig trenches and drill holes into the faults. Then they gather samples of **sediments** that have been deposited and buried over millions of years.

By studying the sediments, scientists can tell whether they have been disrupted by ancient earthquakes. The sediments also provide clues about how frequently the quakes struck and how fast the fault has moved and changed over time. This information helps scientists determine how the faults will likely behave in the future.

One fault that has captured the interest of scientists is located beneath Los Angeles, California. It is known as the Puente Hills Blind Thrust system. **Blind thrust faults** are buried beneath the Earth and are not visible on the surface. Workers drilling for oil discovered the Puente Hills system in 2003. They suspected that it might be a fault and alerted scientists.

By exploring the fault, scientists could tell that the system had a history of earthquakes. In the past

A scientist measures changes in California's San Andreas Fault after a major earthquake.

eleven thousand years, for instance, the Puente Hills area was struck by at least four major quakes. The most recent one occurred in 1987. Although scientists say it was less severe than the ancient quakes, it is a sign that the fault system is active and dangerous. Scientist James Dolan says that is troubling because Los Angeles sits right on top of it. "The good news is that major earthquakes along this fault are very infrequent," he says, "[and] it may not happen again for thousands of years. The bad news is that it could be very strong when it does happen."[6]

The Parkfield Experiment

Scientists know that just believing an earthquake could happen is not enough. They must be able to pinpoint where and when the quake is likely to strike. Paul Lowman, a scientist with the National Aeronautics and Space Administration (NASA), explains: "If you're doing earthquake prediction, you've got to come up with time, place, and magnitude. If you miss any one of those three, you haven't really made much of a prediction."[7]

Even when scientists do make a prediction, it is usually a long-range forecast. They may predict that an earthquake is likely to strike a particular area sometime in the next ten to twenty years. But it is far more challenging to identify regions where quakes will occur tomorrow, next month, or next year. Making such specific predictions can lead to mistakes and false alarms. That is because earthquakes do not strike with any sort of predictable regularity.

Scientists learned firsthand about the unpredictability of earthquakes during a study in Parkfield, California. Often called the "earthquake capital of the world," Parkfield sits atop a highly active section of the San Andreas Fault. From 1857 to 1966, the region experienced strong earthquakes on an average of every twenty two years. Seismograph readings showed that the same areas on the fault had broken apart over and over again. These factors suggested that earthquakes could, in fact, strike with predictability.

In 1985, scientists from the USGS and other organizations began monitoring the fault. They collected data and entered it into complex programs known as **computer models**. Then they determined that a major earthquake would strike Parkfield sometime between 1987 and 1992. By the end of 1993, there was still no sign of the expected quake. When a magnitude 6 earthquake struck in 2004, none of the information the researchers collected

A guide explains to visitors why Parkfield, California, has so many earthquakes.

had predicted it. They realized that there was still much work to do before they could forecast earthquakes with precise accuracy.

"It Is Not Easy"

One scientist who strongly believes that accurate quake prediction is possible is Vladimir Keilis-Borok. He leads a team of scientists from the United States, Russia, Western Europe, Japan, and Canada. The group has correctly predicted a number of earthquakes.

The scientists on Keilis-Borok's team use a combination of data to arrive at their forecasts. They study chains of small earthquakes from the past. They look at these small quakes as signs that major earthquakes will follow. They also consider data about faults, including how they have changed over time. After feeding all the information into computer models, the scientists search for obvious patterns in quake activity. This allows them to determine a probable time and location of a large earthquake in a particular region.

In June 2003 the team forecast that a quake of 6.4 magnitude or higher would occur in central California within nine months. The following December, the area was struck by a magnitude 6.5 earthquake. The scientists also predicted that a major quake would hit Japan before the end of December 2003. In September of that year, a magnitude 8.1 earthquake struck the Japanese island of Hokkaido.

Scientists in Parkfield, California, use laser technology to detect very small movements of the Earth.

The scientists were not so successful a year later, however. They predicted that a large earthquake would strike Southern California before September 5, 2004. The quake never occurred, and as of autumn 2006, there was still no sign of one. Keilis-Borok explains why he and his fellow scientists are not discouraged by their incorrect forecast: "Our team always expected from the start that some of our predictions would be false alarms. [W]e are also confident that many will be correct. . . . If we made no mistakes, it would mean the problem is easy; and it is not easy, to put it mildly."[8]

A scientist points on a map to the epicenter of a 6.5 magnitude quake that struck central California in 2003.

Earthquake prediction has come a long way in recent decades. Although some scientists continue to believe that accurate quake prediction may never become a reality, others insist they are wrong. As Keilis-Borok explains, "Earthquake prediction . . . has been considered impossible by many scientists. It is not impossible."[9] In time, he hopes, scientists worldwide will agree.

Chapter 3

"Wailing Sirens Blare"

There are close ties between earthquake predictions and warnings. The difference between them is that warning systems spring into action after an earthquake has already begun. They are designed to detect movement deep within the Earth before humans can feel the tremors. Then the systems issue alerts that an earthquake is about to happen.

Earthquake warning systems are used in several countries, including Japan, Taiwan, Mexico, and Turkey. Although the United States does not have such a warning system in place, tests began on three experimental systems during the summer of 2006. One of them was developed by Richard Allen, a scientist from the University of California at Berkeley. He explains the value of having such a system: "Early warning isn't a [magical cure-all]. But I do think it can reduce the impacts of earthquakes."[10]

A Land of Earthquakes

Perhaps more than any country on Earth, Japan understands the importance of reducing the impact of earthquakes. Like Indonesia, Japan is an island nation located in the Ring of Fire. Directly beneath it, the Pacific, Philippine, and Eurasian plates come together. These plates are constantly grinding and scraping against each other. This generates a tremendous amount of seismic activity, making Japan one of the most earthquake-prone areas on the planet.

At least 20 percent of the world's magnitude 6 and greater earthquakes occur in Japan. Each year more than a thousand quakes are strong enough to be felt. In 1995 the country experienced its worst earthquake in 50 years. The Great Hanshin-Awaji Earthquake struck near the Japanese city of Kobe, killing nearly 6,000 people.

A far more devastating earthquake struck the capital city of Tokyo on September 1, 1923. Known as the Great Kanto Earthquake, it was one of the worst natural disasters in history. More than 100,000 people were killed, and hundreds of thousands were left homeless.

Because Japan is at such great risk for earthquakes, the country has one of the world's most advanced early-warning systems. It is composed of hundreds of underground sensors installed in key areas along fault lines. When the sensors detect the first tremors of an earthquake, they relay signals to a central computer. It, in turn, is pro-grammed to send out warning signals, as science writer Alicia Chang explains: "Wailing sirens blare that a big one is on its way."[11]

In the event of a warning, disaster response centers, hospitals, factories, and schools are alerted. Nuclear power stations and airport runways are shut down. Workers at construction sites are

Japan's early-warning system for earthquakes is monitored by a scientist.

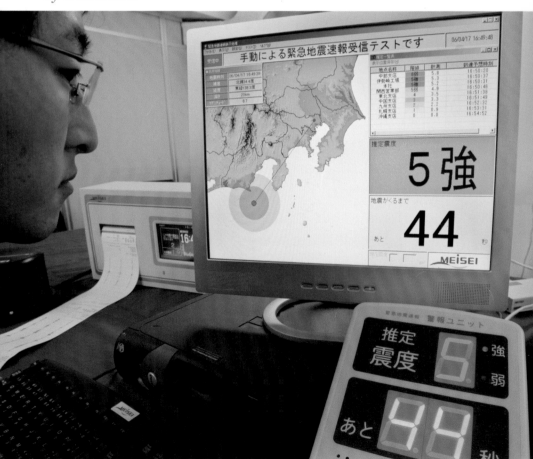

warned to take cover. Japan's railway system head-quarters also receives a warning. If railway officials believe the trains are in danger, they order drivers to immediately make an emergency stop. This occurred in May 2003, when a powerful earthquake struck Tokyo. Warnings caused two high-speed bullet trains to come to a dead stop. If the trains had continued speeding along, they would have crossed a bridge that had been badly cracked by the earthquake. The result could have been tragic.

Every Second Counts

Although warnings can work well in some places, not every region can benefit from them. Areas nearest the **epicenter**, or the point directly above the hypocenter, have little chance of being alerted in time. That is what happened in October 2004, when a magnitude 6.8 earthquake struck the Niigata area of central Japan. The shaking Earth ripped a bullet train from its rails, crumbled buildings, and caused roads to buckle. One second-floor supermarket collapsed, trapping 300 people inside. By the time the earthquake was over, 40 people had been killed and more than 3,000 were injured.

When an earthquake is about to happen, people located farther away from the epicenter have the most time to prepare. But even that warning may arrive less than a minute before the quake strikes. David Wald of the USGS National Earthquake Center in Colorado explains: "When people think

When this early-warning system detects a quake, it alerts Japan's railway system to stop all trains in the area.

of early warning, they think they'll get time to do something useful before shaking starts. But in reality, you don't get a lot of time."[12] Still, many scientists are convinced that even a few precious seconds can mean the difference between life and death.

Making Waves

Whether warning systems provide minutes or seconds of advance notice, the reason they work is because seismic waves travel at different speeds. There are two major types of waves: primary waves (or P waves) and secondary waves (or S waves).

At the earthquake's hypocenter, the P waves are generated first. They are weaker than S waves, and they travel about twice as fast. According to Hiroo Kanamori, a scientist at the California Institute of Technology, "The P waves carry information; the S waves carry energy."[13]

Even with early-warning systems, a major 2004 earthquake derailed this Japanese high-speed bullet train.

When an earthquake warning system is in place, the P waves travel through a network of seismic sensors and arrive at monitoring stations. Scientists quickly analyze the waves to determine when the S waves will be felt and how strong they will be. If the scientists deem that a severe earthquake is about to strike, they send out electronic signals. The signals zoom through wires or air faster than the S waves can move through the Earth. Because of that, the warning can reach automated systems and humans before the full force of the earthquake is felt.

Tsunami Ahead!

One type of warning system alerts coastal areas about an approaching tsunami. The Pacific Tsunami Warning Center in Ewa Beach, Hawaii, is one example. It monitors the Hawaiian Islands and other American territories in the Pacific. It also serves as the International Tsunami Warning Center for twenty-five other countries in the Pacific Ocean Basin. A similar system is in place in Japan, as well as in Alaska. The Alaska Tsunami Warning Center in the city of Palmer serves as the regional warning center for British Columbia, Washington, Oregon, and California, as well as Alaska.

Tsunami warning systems are made up of several different parts that work together. Seismographs monitor earthquake activity and alert scientists if the quake's tremors are strong enough to produce a tsunami. Tidal gauges, which are instruments that

Equipped with a GPS locator, this buoy sends information from deep-sea sensors to warn of an approaching tsunami.

measure sea level, record changes in ocean depth. When a tsunami first forms, powerful seismic energy speeds through the water. This energy can push the water upward above normal sea level. Tidal gauges are able to detect that sort of change.

Sea level is also monitored by deep-sea pressure detectors. These instruments are anchored to the ocean floor. When they sense even a tiny change, they relay the information to large buoys that float on the surface of the water. The buoys have **Global Positioning System** (GPS) antennas mounted on the top. When they receive data from the pressure detectors, they transmit the data to GPS satellites. Then the satellites send signals to warning centers, alerting them that a tsunami is on its way.

Although tsunami and earthquake warning systems are designed to alert people that a natural disaster is about to strike, they are far from perfect. Scientists continue working to improve these systems. Their goal is to develop methods of prediction and warning so advanced that they will minimize damage and save human lives.

Chapter 4

Earthquake Prediction in the Future

Earthquakes are such powerful forces of nature that there is nothing anyone can do to stop them. But scientists constantly search for ways to more accurately predict quakes, as well as develop improved warning systems. John Rundle, a scientist at the University of California, Davis, explains: "We can't prevent these devastating events, but we can provide tools so that people can take steps to reduce the potential damage and loss of life."[14]

Finding Hot Spots

For scientists to develop those tools, they must continue to learn as much as possible about how and why earthquakes occur. A key step is broadening their knowledge about Earth's major fault systems. A greater understanding of faults can help scientists become better at pinpointing the world's danger zones, which are often called hot spots.

Huge gashes mar cultivated rice fields along Japan's Nojima Fault.

Once hot spots have been identified, scientists develop worldwide charts known as hazard maps. Even if they cannot predict earthquakes with precise accuracy, they can use hazard maps to inform the public about where quakes are most likely to strike. These maps have been compared to charts of dangerous traffic intersections. USGS seismic mapping architect Art Frankel explains: "They can't predict when the next car accident will happen, but they do tell you to watch out."[15]

Making the Public Aware

Educating people about danger zones is only one way to teach them how to protect themselves against earthquakes. Many countries offer formal earthquake education programs. In Japan, for instance, schoolchildren learn about earthquake safety in the classroom. At the Nakamachi Elementary School in Sendai, Japan, students participate in regular earthquake drills. They are taught to duck under their desks to avoid being struck by falling ceiling tiles, light fixtures, and other objects. Teachers also participate in the drills. They learn emergency procedures, such as opening classroom doors if an earthquake warning sounds. This prevents the doors from jamming shut, which could hinder an emergency evacuation.

Another aspect of earthquake education is making people in coastal areas aware that earthquakes can trigger tsunamis. The main reason why the 2004 Indian Ocean tsunami claimed so many lives is because people were not prepared for it. They did not know about warning signs such as a rapid change in sea level. In the island country of Sri Lanka, for instance, the ocean rose 15 feet (4.6m) in less than one minute. It rushed back out, and then an enormous wall of water slammed into the Sri Lankan shoreline.

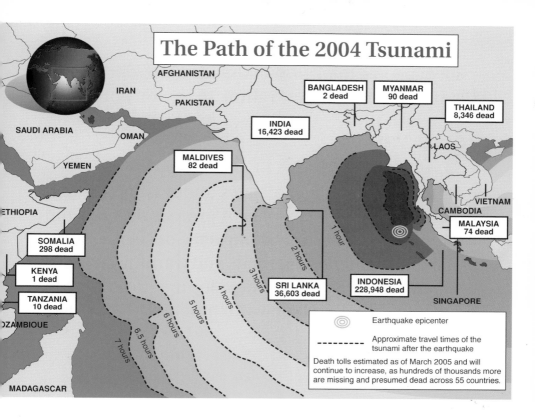

The Path of the 2004 Tsunami

AFGHANISTAN

IRAN

PAKISTAN

SAUDI ARABIA

OMAN

YEMEN

ETHIOPIA

SOMALIA
298 dead

KENYA
1 dead

TANZANIA
10 dead

MOZAMBIQUE

MADAGASCAR

BANGLADESH
2 dead

MYANMAR
90 dead

THAILAND
8,346 dead

INDIA
16,423 dead

LAOS

MALDIVES
82 dead

VIETNAM

CAMBODIA

MALAYSIA
74 dead

SRI LANKA
36,603 dead

INDONESIA
228,948 dead

SINGAPORE

1 hour
2 hours
3 hours
4 hours
5 hours
6 hours
6.5 hours
7 hours

◎ Earthquake epicenter

- - - - - Approximate travel times of the
tsunami after the earthquake

Death tolls estimated as of March 2005 and will
continue to increase, as hundreds of thousands more
are missing and presumed dead across 55 countries.

In coastal regions of the United States, public officials conduct education programs about tsunamis. One of those programs takes place in the state of Washington. Scientists have determined that towns such as Ocean Shores are at risk of being hit by a tsunami. Yet the people who live in Ocean Shores, as well as tourists who visit, have not always taken that risk seriously. In fact, when blue and white tsunami warning signs were posted around the town, people stole them as souvenirs! After the 2004 Indian Ocean tsunami, however, the public's attitude changed. They realized just how dangerous tsunamis can be. According to Tim Walsh, a hazards program manager in Washington, this was an important lesson for people all over the world. "A lot of people think of tsunamis as some kind of cool adventure," he says. "I think they won't be doing that next time."[16]

The Power of Technology

Educating people of all ages about tsunamis and earthquakes is a key part of protecting lives and property. Equally important is the development of reliable prediction methods and warning systems. Scientists at NASA are developing a number of advanced tools to help with these tasks. One pow-

A seismologist shows what the force of the 2004 Indian Ocean tsunami looked like on a seismograph.

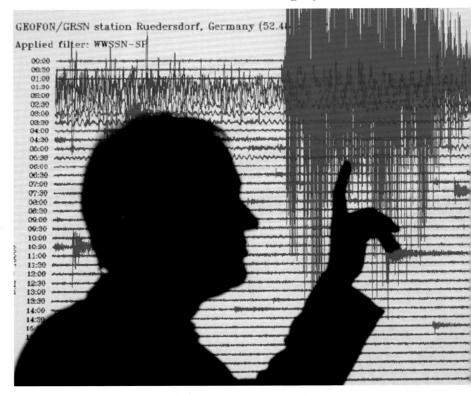

erful high-tech program is called QuakeSim, which NASA hopes will be in use by about 2010. QuakeSim involves placing GPS receivers along fault lines and in other critical locations. Scientists will monitor the signals that the receivers transmit to GPS satellites. They will be able to tell when a tectonic plate has moved and in which direction it is heading. They will also be able to determine how fast the plate is moving.

Another part of the QuakeSim project is known as InSAR. It uses radar equipment mounted on satellites to detect tiny motions deep within the Earth. The radar equipment is so sensitive that scientists will be able to see land changes around fault lines in more detail than ever before. Science writer Jim Wilson says that InSAR can be compared to "an **orbiting** version of the speed gun state troopers use to clock speeders."[17] By watching these changes, scientists will be able to determine where points of high strain are building up.

Scientists hope QuakeSim and other technology will help them spot the signs of an earthquake days or weeks before it strikes. That would give the public and emergency planners time to prepare for an approaching disaster.

Smarter Structures

Just as scientists seek better ways to monitor earthquake activity, they continuously work toward protecting people against them. One of the most important things they can do is develop structures that withstand a quake's violent shaking.

During an earthquake, natural hazards such as landslides can be deadly, but they are not the greatest risk. The most common cause of injury and death is the collapse of major structures. In October 1989, for instance, a powerful earthquake struck the California town of Loma Prieta. The Cypress Viaduct, a raised freeway with two traffic decks, was severely damaged by the quake. This caused the

The two-tiered Cypress Viaduct in Oakland, California, collapsed during the 1989 Loma Prieta earthquake.

upper roadway to slam down on the lower road, killing forty-two people. Investigators later determined that the support frames of the viaduct had been built on weak soil. When the ground started shaking, huge cracks formed in the frames. This weakened the structure and caused it to collapse.

Buildings are also in danger of crumbling during earthquakes. This is especially true in poor, developing nations where there are no strict building codes and standards. In countries such as India, Thailand, Malaysia, and Mexico, buildings are often poorly constructed. Science writer Mark Zoback describes such structures as "death traps waiting to happen." He says even a small amount of shaking is enough to topple buildings into piles of rubble. As he explains: "One image imprinted on my mind is that of relief workers standing atop a once six-story building in Mexico City that was literally pancaked in 1978 by an earthquake 200 miles away."[18]

Earthquake-Proof Buildings

Throughout the world, architects and engineers are designing buildings to be as earthquake proof as possible. They use superstrong materials that can bend, stretch, and compress without breaking. One unique system was developed by scientists at Lehigh University in Pennsylvania. It features gigantic ropelike steel bands that hold a building's frame together. During a quake the bands allow beams and columns the flexibility to rock, twist,

A survivor of the 2006 Indonesian earthquake sits stunned amid the devastation.

and separate. This keeps the frame from buckling. When the tremors stop, the bands pull the beams and columns back to their original positions.

By combining knowledge, technology, and stronger construction methods, scientists hope they can prevent future earthquakes from causing as much devastation as past quakes. As science writer Tom Harris explains: "Just like severe weather and disease, earthquakes are an unavoidable force generated by the powerful natural processes that shape our planet. All we can do is increase our understanding and . . . develop better ways to deal with it."[19]

Chapter 1: Nature's Violence

1. Crystal Wicker, "Earthquakes," *Weather Wiz Kids*. www.weatherwizkids.com/earthquake1.htm.
2. United States Geological Survey Hawaiian Volcano Observatory, "Indonesia Pays Heavy Price for Proximity to Plate Boundary," June 8, 2006. http://hvo.wr.usgs.gov/volcanowatch/current_issue.html.
3. Quoted in Daniel Pendick, "Quake Prediction," PBS Online, *Savage Earth—The Restless Planet: Earthquakes*. www.wnet.org/savageearth/earthquakes/html/sidebar2.html.

Chapter 2: A Challenging Science

4. Quoted in John Roach, "Earthquake Prediction Remains a Moving Target," *National Geographic News*, July 14, 2004. http://news.nationalgeographic.com/news/2004/07/0714_040714_earthquakeprediction.html.
5. Quoted in PhysOrg.com, "Scientists Issue Indonesia Earthquake Warning," *Space and Earth Science*, March 17, 2005. www.physorg.com/news3422.html.
6. Quoted in Stefan Lovgren, "Newfound L.A. Fault Threatens Major Quake," *National Geographic News*, April 3, 2003. http://news.nationalgeographic.com/news/2003/04/0403_030403_earthquake.html.
7. Quoted in Leonard David, "Earthquake Forecasting, Satellite System May Provide Warning," Space.com, July 12, 2002. www.space.com/scienceastronomy/earthquake_watch_020712.html.
8. Quoted in Naomi Lubick, "Botched Earthquake Prediction," *Geotimes*, September 7, 2004. www.agiweb.org/geotimes/sept04/WebExtra090704.html#.

9. Quoted in Dave Downey, "Forecast Has Attention of Earthquake Experts," *NC Times.com*, June 12, 2004. www.nctimes.com/articles/2004/06/13/news/top_stories/19_33_536_12_04.txt.

Chapter 3: "Wailing Sirens Blare"

10. Quoted in Alicia Chang, "U.S. Quake Warning Systems Lag," *Wired News*, May 28, 2006. www.wired.com/news/wireservice/0,71019-0.html?tw=wn_index_5.
11. Quoted in Chang, "U.S. Quake Warning Systems Lag."
12. Quoted in Chang, "U.S. Quake Warning Systems Lag."
13. Quoted in Dennis Normile, "Earthquake Preparedness: Some Countries Are Betting That a Few Seconds Can Save Lives," *Science*, December 24, 2004, p. 2178.

Chapter 4: Earthquake Prediction in the Future

14. Quoted in "Tsunami Earthquake Location Included in Forecast," *UC Davis News & Information*, December 29, 2004. www.news.ucdavis.edu/search/news_detail.lasso?id=7237.
15. Quoted in Kevin Krajick, "Future Shocks: Modern Science, Ancient Catastrophes and the Endless Quest to Predict Earthquakes," *Smithsonian*, March 2005, p. 38.
16. Quoted in Krajick, "Future Shocks: Modern Science, Ancient Catastrophes and the Endless Quest to Predict Earthquakes."
17. Jim Wilson, "Predicting Earthquakes from Space," *Popular Mechanics*, December 16, 2003. www.popularmechanics.com/science/space/1282866.html.
18. Mark Zoback, "Earthquake Prediction and the Developing World," *Geotimes*, March 2004. www.agiweb.org/geotimes/mar04/comment.html.
19. Tom Harris, "How Earthquakes Work," *HowStuffWorks*. (http://science.howstuffworks.com/earthquake.htm).

Glossary

blind thrust faults: Faults that are deep within the Earth and not visible on the surface.

computer models: Complex computer programs that scientists use to help predict earthquakes and other natural phenomena.

crust: Earth's rigid top layer.

epicenter: The point on the Earth's surface immediately above where an earthquake is generated.

faults: Cracks in the Earth's crust that are caused by the movement of tectonic plates.

Global Positioning System (GPS): A worldwide system that uses satellite signals to track the location of people or objects on Earth.

hypocenter: The source of an earthquake.

orbiting: Circling the Earth.

paleoseismology: The study of past earthquakes.

plate tectonics: The scientific theory that Earth's crust is divided into about twelve gigantic chunks, known as plates, that float on the mantle.

Richter scale: The system used to measure an earthquake's magnitude.

sediments: Soil, sand, or other particles deposited by wind or water.

seismic: Having to do with shock waves in the Earth caused by earthquakes.

seismographs: Instruments that detect and record the vibrations of an earthquake.

subduction: The process of one tectonic plate being shoved beneath another.

tsunami: An enormous and powerful sea wave caused by an underwater earthquake or other violent disturbance in the Earth.

For Further Exploration

Books

Seymour Simon, *Earthquakes*. New York: HarperCollins, 2006. This book examines how earthquakes form, what tectonic plates are, where earthquakes are most common, the disastrous damage they can cause, and how they can be predicted.

Susanna Van Rose, *Volcanoes and Earthquakes*. New York: Dorling Kindersley, 2004. Enhanced by colorful photographs and illustrations, this book explains how volcanoes and earthquakes occur by carefully examining the science behind these natural disasters.

Periodicals

"Aftershock: Rebuilding After Southern Asia's Earthquake," *Weekly Reader*, November 18, 2005.

"Earthquake: Nature's Fury," *Children's World*, January 2002.

"On the Richter Scale," *Crinkles*, March/April 2002.

Internet Sources

Renee Skelton, "Earthquake!" *National Geographic Kids Magazine*, March 2004. www.nationalgeographic.com/ngkids/0403/main.html.

Katheryn Troyer, "Predicting Earthquakes," *KidsNewsRoom*, December 10, 2004. www.kidsnewsroom.org.

Web Sites

HowStuffWorks (www.howstuffworks.com). Includes several detailed sections and well-written information related to earthquakes, including "How Earthquakes Work" and "How Tsunamis Work."

National Geographic, Forces of Nature: Earthquakes (www.nationalgeographic.com/forcesofnature/earthquakes.html). This site explains what causes earthquakes, where they most often occur, and how they are measured. Also features case studies of some of the most disastrous earthquakes, as well as an interactive "Make your own quake" feature.

Index